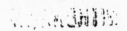

THE DESERT MUSIC AND OTHER POEMS

THE DESERT MUSIC

AND OTHER POEMS, BY

WILLIAM CARLOS WILLIAMS

RANDOM HOUSE · NEW YORK

MANUFACTURED IN THE UNITED STATES OF AMERICA

THE SPIRAL PRESS · NEW YORK

TO BILL AND PAUL

CONTENTS

PART ONE

THE DESERT MUSIC AND OTHER POEMS

THE DESCENT

The descent beckons
        as the ascent beckoned.
           Memory is a kind
of accomplishment,
      a sort of renewal
         even
an initiation, since the spaces it opens are new places
      inhabited by hordes
         heretofore unrealized,
of new kinds —
     since their movements
        are towards new objectives
(even though formerly they were abandoned).

NO DEFEAT is made up entirely of defeat — since
the world it opens is always a place
    formerly
       unsuspected.   A
world lost,
    a world unsuspected,
       beckons to new places
and no whiteness (lost) is so white as the memory
of whiteness   .

WITH EVENING, love wakens
  though its shadows
    which are alive by reason
of the sun shining —
  grow sleepy now and drop away
    from desire .

LOVE WITHOUT shadows stirs now
  beginning to awaken
    as night
advances.

THE DESCENT
  made up of despairs
    and without accomplishment
realizes a new awakening:
    which is a reversal
of despair.
    For what we cannot accomplish, what
is denied to love,
  what we have lost in the anticipation —
    a descent follows,
endless and indestructible .

TO DAPHNE
AND VIRGINIA

THE SMELL OF the heat is boxwood
when rousing us
a movement of the air
stirs our thoughts
that had no life in them
to a life, a life in which
two women agonize:
to live and to breathe is no less.
Two young women.
The box odor
is the odor of that of which
partaking separately,
each to herself
I partake also
.   .   separately.

BE PATIENT THAT I address you in a poem,
there is no other
fit medium.
The mind
lives there. It is uncertain,
can trick us and leave us

agonized. But for resources
        what can equal it?
               There is nothing. We
should be lost
        without its wings to
            fly off upon.
THE MIND IS the cause of our distresses
        but of it we can build anew.
               Oh something more than
it flies off to:
        a woman's world,
            of crossed sticks, stopping
thought. A new world
        is only a new mind.
             And the mind and the poem
are all apiece.
        Two young women
            to be snared,
odor of box,
        to bind and hold them
            for the mind's labors.

ALL WOMEN ARE fated similarly
        facing men
               and there is always
another, such as I,
        who loves them,
               loves all women, but
finds himself, touching them,
        like other men,
               often confused.

I HAVE TWO sons,
        the husbands of these women,
           who live also
in a world of love,
        apart.
               Shall this odor of box in
               the heat
not also touch them
        fronting a world of women
           from which they are
debarred
        by the very scents which draw them on
           against easy access?

IN OUR FAMILY we stammer unless,
half mad,
we come to speech at last   .

AND I AM not
a young man.
My love encumbers me.
It is a love
less than
a young man's love but,
like this box odor
more penetrant, infinitely
more penetrant,
in that sense not to be resisted.

THERE IS, IN the hard
give and take
of a man's life with
a woman
a thing which is not the stress itself
but beyond
and above

that,

        something that wants to rise

           and shake itself

free. We are not chickadees

        on a bare limb

           with a worm in the mouth.

The worm is in our brains

        and concerns them

           and not food for our

offspring, wants to disrupt

        our thought

           and throw it

to the newspapers

        or anywhere.

           There is, in short,

a counter stress,

        born of the sexual shock,

           which survives it

consonant with the moon,

        to keep its own mind.

           There is, of course,

more.

Women

are not alone

in that. At least

while this healing odor is abroad

one can write a poem.

STAYING HERE in the country

on an old farm

we eat our breakfasts

on a balcony under an elm.

The shrubs below us

are neglected. And

there, penned in,

or he would eat the garden,

lives a pet goose who

tilts his head

sidewise

and looks up at us,

a very quiet old fellow

who writes no poems.

Fine mornings we sit there

while birds

     come and go.

          A pair of robins

is building a nest   .

     for the second time

          this season. Men

against their reason

     speak of love, sometimes,

          when they are old. It is

all they can do   .

     or watch a heavy goose

          who waddles, slopping

          noisily in the mud of

          his pool.

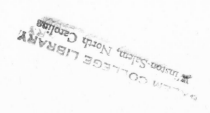

THE ORCHESTRA

The precise counterpart
        of a cacophony of bird calls
                lifting the sun almighty
into his sphere: wood-winds
        clarinet and violins
                sound a prolonged A!
Ah! the sun, the sun! is about to rise
        and shed his beams
                as he has always done
upon us all,
        drudges and those
                who live at ease,
women and men,
        upon the old,
                upon children and the sick
who are about to die and are indeed
        dead in their beds,
                to whom his light
is forever lost. The cello
        raises his bass note
                manfully in the treble din:
Ah, ah and ah!
        together, unattuned
                seeking a common tone.

Love is that common tone

        shall raise his fiery head

              and sound his note.

THE PURPOSE OF an orchestra

        is to organize those sounds

           and hold them

to an assembled order   .

        in spite of the

              "wrong note". Well, shall we

think or listen? Is there a sound addressed

        not wholly to the ear?

          We half close

our eyes. We do not

        hear it through our eyes.

          It is not

a flute-note either, it is the relation

        of a flute-note

             to a drum. I am wide

awake. The mind

        is listening. The ear

           is alerted. But the ear

in a half reluctant mood

    stretches

        .   .   and yawns.

AND SO THE banked violins

    in three tiers

        enliven the scene,

pizzicato. For a short

    memory or to

        make the listener listen

the theme is repeated

    stressing a variant:

        it is a principle of music

to repeat the theme. Repeat

    and repeat again,

        as the pace mounts. The

theme is difficult   .

    but no more difficult

        than the facts to be

resolved. Repeat

    and repeat the theme

        and all it develops to be

until thought is dissolved

in tears.

Our dreams

have been assaulted

by a memory that will not

sleep. The

French horns

interpose

.   .   their voices:

I love you. My heart

is innocent. And this

the first day of the world!

SAY TO THEM:

"Man has survived hitherto because he was too ignorant
to know how to realize his wishes. Now that he can realize
them, he must either change them or perish."

NOW IS THE time   .

in spite of the "wrong note"

I love you. My heart is

innocent.

And this the first

(and last) day of the world

THE BIRDS TWITTER now anew
    but a design
        surmounts their twittering.
It is a design of a man
    that makes them twitter.
      It is a design.

MOTHER OF GOD! Our Lady!
>   the heart
>   is an unruly Master:
Forgive us our sins
>   as we
>   forgive
those who have sinned against
>   us.
>   We submit ourselves
to Your rule
>   as the flowers in May
>   submit themselves to
>   Your Holy rule — against
that impossible spring-time
>   when men
>   shall be the flowers
spread at your feet.

AS FAR AS spring is
>   from winter
>   so are we

from you now. We have not come

easily

to your environs

but painfully

across sands

that have scored our

feet. That which we have suffered

was for us

to suffer. Now,

in the winter of the year,

the birds who know how

to escape suffering

by flight

are gone. Man alone

is that creature who

cannot escape suffering

by flight   .

I DO NOT come to you

save that I confess

to being

half man and half

woman. I have seen the ivy
        cling
                to a piece of crumbled
wall so that
        you cannot tell
           by which either
stands: this is to say
        if she to whom I cling
           is loosened both
of us go down.

MOTHER OF GOD
        I have seen you stoop
           to a merest flower
and raise it
        and press it to your cheek.
           I could have called out
joyfully
        but you were too far off.
           You are a woman and
it was
        a woman's gesture.
           I declare it boldly

with my heart
> in my teeth
>> and my knees knocking

together. Yet I declare
> it, and by God's word
>> it is no lie. Make us

humble and obedient to His rule.

THERE ARE MEN
> who as they live
>> fling caution to the

wind and women praise them
> and love them for it.
>> Cruel as the claws of

a cat   .   .

YOU HAVE NO lover now
> in the bare skies
>> to bring you flowers,

to whisper
> to you under a hedge
>> howbeit

you are young
> and fit to be loved   .

THE MOON WHICH
> they have vulgarized recently
>> is still

your planet
> as it was Venus' before
>> you. What

do they think they will attain
> by their ships
>> that death has not

already given
> them? Their ships
>> should be directed

inward upon   .   But I
> am an old man. I
>> have had enough.

THE FEMALE PRINCIPLE of the world
> is my appeal
>> in the extremity

to which I have come.
> *O clemens! O pia! O dolcis!*
> *Maria!*

TO A DOG INJURED
IN THE STREET

IT IS MYSELF,

      not the poor beast lying there

          yelping with pain

that brings me to myself with a start —

      as at the explosion

          of a bomb, a bomb that has laid

all the world waste.

      I can do nothing

          but sing about it

and so I am assuaged

      from my pain.

A DROWSY NUMBNESS drowns my sense

      as if of hemlock

          I had drunk. I think

of the poetry

      of René Char

          and all he must have seen

and suffered

      that has brought him

          to speak only of

sedgy rivers,
        of daffodils and tulips
            whose roots they water,
even to the freeflowing river
        that laves the rootlets
            of those sweet scented flowers
that people the
        milky
           way   .

I REMEMBER *Norma*
        our English setter of my childhood
            her silky ears
and expressive eyes.
        She had a litter
            of pups one night
in our pantry and I kicked
        one of them
            thinking, in my alarm,
that they
        were biting her breasts
            to destroy her.

I REMEMBER also
> a dead rabbit
>> lying harmlessly
on the outspread palm
> of a hunter's hand.
>> As I stood by
watching
> he took a hunting knife
>> and with a laugh
thrust it
> up into the animal's private parts.
>> I almost fainted.

WHY SHOULD I think of that now?
> The cries of a dying dog
>> are to be blotted out
as best I can.
> René Char
>> you are a poet who believes
in the power of beauty
> to right all wrongs.
>> I believe it also.

With invention and courage
       we shall surpass
              the pitiful dumb beasts,
let all men believe it,
       as you have taught me also
           to believe it.

THE YELLOW FLOWER

WHAT SHALL I say, because talk I must?
        That I have found a cure
                for the sick?
I have found no cure
        for the sick   .
                but this crooked flower
which only to look upon
        all men
                are cured. This
is that flower
        for which all men
                sing secretly their hymns
of praise. This
        is that sacred
                flower!

CAN THIS BE so?
        A flower so crooked
                and obscure? It is
a mustard flower
        and not a mustard flower,
                a single spray

topping the deformed stem
       of fleshy leaves
            in this freezing weather
under glass.

AN UNGAINLY FLOWER and
       an unnatural one,
            in this climate; what
can be the reason
       that it has picked me out
            to hold me, open mouthed,
rooted before this window
       in the cold,
            my will
drained from me
       so that I have only eyes
            for these yellow,
twisted petals   .   ?

THAT THE SIGHT,
       though strange to me,
            must be a common one,

is clear: there are such flowers
    with such leaves
        native to some climate
which they can call
    their own.

BUT WHY THE torture
    and the escape through
        the flower? It is
as if Michelangelo
    had conceived the subject
        of his *Slaves* from this
— or might have done so.
    And did he not make
        the marble bloom? I
am sad
    as he was sad
        in his heroic mood.
But also
    I have eyes
        that are made to see and if
they see ruin for myself
    and all that I hold
        dear, they see

also

  through the eyes

    and through the lips

and tongue the power

    to free myself

      and speak of it, as

Michelangelo through his hands

    had the same, if greater,

      power.

WHICH LEAVES, to account for,

    the tortured bodies

      of

the slaves themselves

    and

          the tortured body of my flower

which is not a mustard flower at all

    but some unrecognized

      and unearthly flower

for me to naturalize

    and acclimate

      and choose it for my own

THE HOST

ACCORDING TO THEIR need,
        this tall Negro evangelist
                (at a separate table from the
                rest of the party);
these two young Irish nuns
        (to be described subsequently);
                and this white-haired Anglican
have come witlessly
        to partake of the host
                laid for them (and for me)
by the tired waitresses.

IT IS ALL
        (since eat we must)
                made sacred by our common need.
The evangelist's assistants
        are most open in their praise
                though covert
as would be seemly
        in such a public
                place. The nuns
are all black, a side view.
        The cleric,
                his head bowed to reveal

his unruly poll
                dines alone.

MY EYES ARE RESTLESS.
                The evangelists eat well,
                                fried oysters and what not
at this railway restaurant. The Sisters
                are soon satisfied. One
                                on leaving,
looking straight before her under steadfast brows,
                reveals
                                blue eyes. I myself
have brown eyes
                and a milder mouth.

THERE IS NOTHING TO eat,
                seek it where you will,
                                but of the body of the Lord.
The blessed plants
                and the sea, yield it
                                to the imagination
intact. And by that force
                it becomes real,
                                bitterly

to the poor animals

who suffer and die

that we may live.

THE WELL-FED EVANGELS,

the narrow lipped and bright eyed nuns,

the tall,

white haired Anglican,

proclaim it by their appetites

as do I also,

chomping with my worn out teeth:

the Lord is my shepherd

I shall not want.

NO MATTER HOW WELL we are fed,

how daintily

we put the food to our lips,

it is all

according to the imagination!

Say what you will of it,

only the imagination

is real! They have imagined it,

therefore it is so:

of the Evangels,

with the long legs characteristic of the race —

only the docile women

of the party smiled at me

when, with my eyes

I accosted them.

The nuns — but after all

I saw only a face, a young face

cut off at the brows.

It was a simple story.

The cleric, plainly

from a good school,

interested me more,

a man with whom I might

carry on a conversation.

NO ONE WAS there

save only for

the food. Which I alone,

being a poet,

could have given them.

But I

had only my eyes

with which to speak.

DEEP RELIGIOUS FAITH

Past death
        past rainy days
                or the distraction
of Lady Smocks all silver-white;
        beyond the remote borders
                of poetry itself
if it does not drive us,
        it is vain.
                Yet it is
that which made El Greco
        paint his green and distorted saints
                and live
lean.
        It is what in life drives us
                to praise music
and the old
        or sit by a friend
                in his last hours.

ALL THAT WHICH makes the pear ripen
        or the poet's line
                come true!
Invention is the heart of it.

WITHOUT THE QUIRKS
>> and oddnesses of invention
>>>> the paralytic is confirmed
> in his paralysis,
>> it is from a northern
>>> and half savage country
> where the religion
>> is hate.
>>> There
the citizens are imprisoned.
>> The rose
>>> may not be worshipped
or the poet look to it
>> for benefit.

IN THE NIGHT a
>> storm of gale proportions came
>> up.
>>> No one was there to envisage
a field of daisies!
>> There were bellowings
>>> and roarings

from a child's book
       of fairy tales,
              the rumble
of a distant bombing
       — or a bee!
              Shame on our poets,
they have caught the prevalent fever:
       impressed
              by the "laboratory,"
they have forgot
       the flower!
              which goes beyond all
laboratories!
       They have quit the job
              of invention. The
imagination has fallen asleep
       in a poppy-cup.

THE GARDEN

IT IS FAR TO ASSISI,
        but not too far:
                Over this garden,
brooding over this garden,
        there is a kindly spirit,
                brother to the poor
and who is poorer than he
        who is in love
                when birds are nesting
in the spring of the year?
        They came
                to eat from his hand
who had nothing,
        and yet
                from his plenty
he fed them all.
        All mankind
                grew to be his debtors,
a simple story.
        Love is in season.

AT SUCH A TIME,
        hyacinth time
                in

the hospital garden,
> the time
>> of the coral flowered

and early salmon pink
> clusters, it is
>> the time also of

abandoned birds' nests
> before
>> the sparrows start

>> to tear them apart

against the advent of that bounty
> from which
>> they will build anew.

ALL ABOUT THEM
> on the lawns
>> the young couples

embrace   .
> as in a tale
>> by Boccaccio

They are careless
> under license of the disease
>> which has restricted them

to these grounds.
         St. Francis forgive them
            and all lovers
whoever they may be.
         They have seen
            a great light, it
springs from their own bawdy foreheads.
         The light
            is sequestered there
by these enclosing walls.
         They are divided
            from their fellows.
It is a bounty
         from last year's nest.
         St. Francis,
who befriended the wild birds,
         by their aid,
            those who
have nothing,
         and live
            by the Holy light of love
that rules,
         blocking despair,
            over this garden.

TIME PASSES.
> The pace has slackened
>> But with the falling off

of the pace
> the scene has altered.
>> The lovers raise their heads,

at that which has come over them.
> It is summer now.
>> The broad sun

shines!
> Blinded by the light
>> they walk bewildered,

seeking
> between the leaves
>> for a vantage

from which to view
> the advancing season.
>> They are incredulous

of their own cure
> and half minded
>> to escape

into the dark again.
> The scene
>> indeed has changed.

By St. Francis
> the whole scene
>> has changed.

They glimpse
> a surrounding sky
>> and the whole countryside.

Filled with terror
> they seek
>> a familiar flower

at which to warm themselves,
> but the whole field
>> accosts them.

They hide their eyes
> ashamed
>> before that bounty,

peering through their fingers
> timidly.
>> The saint is watching,

his eyes filled with pity.

THE YEAR IS STILL young
> but not so young
>> as they

who face the fears

    with which

        they are confronted.

Reawakened

    after love's first folly

        they resemble children

roused from a long sleep.

    Summer is here,

        right enough.

The saint

    has tactfully withdrawn.

        One

emboldened,

    parting the leaves before her,

        stands in the full sunlight,

alone

    shading her eyes

        as her heart

beats wildly

    and her mind

        drinks up

the full meaning

    of it

        all!

THE ARTIST

Mr. T.
> bareheaded
>> in a soiled undershirt
his hair standing out
> on all sides
>> stood on his toes
heels together
> arms gracefully
>> for the moment
curled above his head.
> Then he whirled about
>> bounded
into the air
> and with an *entrechat*
>> perfectly achieved
completed the figure.
> My mother
>> taken by surprise
where she sat
> in her invalid's chair
>> was left speechless.
Bravo! she cried at last
> and clapped her hands.
>> The man's wife

came from the kitchen:

What goes on here? she said.

But the show was over.

WORK IN PROGRESS

Of asphodel, that greeny flower,
>   like a buttercup
>   upon its branching stem —
save that it's green and wooden —
>   I come, my sweet,
>   to sing to you.
We lived long together
>   a life filled,
>   if you will,
with flowers. So that
>   I was cheered
>   when I came first to know
that there were flowers also
>   in hell.
>   Today
I'm filled with the fading memory of those flowers
>   that we both loved,
>   even to this poor
colorless thing —
>   I saw it
>   when I was a child —
little prized among the living
>   but the dead see,
>   asking among themselves:

What do I remember
     that was shaped
         as this thing is shaped?
while our eyes fill
     with tears.
         Of love, abiding love
it will be telling
     tho' too weak a wash of crimson
         colors it
to make it wholly credible.
     There is something
         something urgent
I have to say to you
     and you alone   .
         but it must wait
while I drink in
     the joy of your approach,
         perhaps for the last time.
And so
     with fear in my heart
         I drag it out
and keep on talking
     for I dare not stop.
         Listen while I talk on

against time.

      It will not be

         for long.

I have forgot   .

      and yet I see clearly enough

         something

central to the sky

      which ranges round it.

         An odor

springs from it!

      A sweetest odor!

         Honeysuckle! And now

there comes the buzzing of a bee!

      and a whole flood

         of sister memories!

Only give me time,

      time to recall them

         before I shall speak out.

Give me time,

      time.

When I was a boy

      I kept a book

         to which, from time

to time,

        I added pressed flowers

                until, after a time,

I had a good collection.

        The asphodel,

                forebodingly,

among them.

        I bring you,

                reawakened,

a memory of those flowers.

        They were sweet

                when I pressed them

and retained

        something of their sweetness

                a long time.

It is a curious odor,

        a moral odor,

                that brings me

near to you.

        The color

                was the first to go.

There had come to me

        a challenge,

                your dear self,

mortal as I was,

the lily's throat

to the hummingbird!

Endless wealth,

I thought,

held out its arms to me.

A thousand tropics

in an apple blossom.

The generous earth itself

gave us lieve.

The whole world

became my garden!

But the sea

which no one tends

is also a garden

when the sun strikes it

and the waves

are wakened.

I have seen it

and so have you

when it puts all flowers

to shame.

Too, there are the starfish

stiffened by the sun

and other sea wrack

and weeds. We knew that

along with the rest of it

for we were born by the sea,

knew its rose hedges

to the very water's edge.

There the pink mallow grows

and in their season

strawberries

and there, later,

we went to gather

the wild plum.

I cannot say

that I have gone to hell

for your love

but often

found myself there

in your pursuit.

I do not like it

and wanted to be

in heaven. Hear me out.

Do not turn away.

I have learned much in my life
   from books
     and out of them
about love.
   Death
     is not the end of it.
There is a hierarchy
   which can be obtained,
     I think,
in its service.
   Its guerdon
     is a fairy flower;
a cat of twenty lives.
   If no one came to try it
    the world
would be the loser.
   It has been
     for you and me
as one who watches a storm
   come in over the water.
     We have stood
from year to year
   before the spectacle of our lives
     with joined hands.

The storm unfolds.

    Lightning

        plays about the edges of the clouds

The sky to the north

    is placid,

        blue in the afterglow

as the storm piles up.

    It is a flower

        that will soon reach

the apex of its bloom.

    We danced,

        in our minds,

and read a book together.

    You remember?

        It was a serious book.

And so books

    entered our lives.

The sea! The sea!

    Always

        when I think of the sea

there comes to mind

    the Iliad

        and Helen's public fault

that bred it.

Were it not for that

there would have been

no poem but the world

if we had remembered,

those crimson petals

spilled among the stones,

would have called it simply

murder.

The sexual orchid that bloomed then

sending so many

disinterested

men to their graves

has left its memory

to a race of fools

or heroes

if silence is a virtue.

The sea alone

with its multiplicity

holds any hope.

The storm

has proven abortive

but we remain

after the thoughts it roused

to

       recement our lives.

          It is the mind

the mind

       that must be cured

          short of death's

intervention,

       and the will becomes again

          a garden. The poem

is complex and the place made

       in our lives

          for the poem.

Silence can be complex too,

       but you do not get far

          with silence.

Begin again.

       It is like Homer's

          catalogue of ships:

it fills up the time.

       I speak in figures,

          well enough, the dresses

you wear are figures also,

       we could not meet

          otherwise. When I speak

of flowers

       it is to recall

        that at one time

we were young.

       All women are not Helen,

         I know that,

but have Helen in their hearts.

       My sweet,

          you have it also, therefore

I love you

       and could not love you otherwise.

        Imagine you saw

a field made up of women

       all silver-white.

        What should you do

but love them?

       The storm bursts

         or fades! it is not

the end of the world.

       Love is something else,

         or so I thought it,

a garden which expands,

       though I knew you as a woman

         and never thought otherwise,

until the whole sea

    has been taken up

        and all its gardens.

It was the love of love,

    the love that swallows up all else,

        a grateful love,

a love of nature, of people,

    animals,

        a love engendering

gentleness and goodness

    that moved me

        and *that* I saw in you.

I should have known,

    though I did not,

        that the lily-of-the-valley

is a flower makes many ill

    who whiff it.

        We had our children,

rivals in the general onslaught.

    I put them aside

        though I cared for them

as well as any man

    could care for his children

        according to my lights.

You understand

        I had to meet you

                after the event

and have still to meet you.

        Love

                to which you too shall bow

along with me —

        a flower

                a weakest flower

shall be our trust

        and not because

                we are too feeble

to do otherwise

        but because

                at the height of my power

I risked what I had to do,

        therefore to prove

                that we love each other

while my very bones sweated

        that I could not cry to you

                in the act.

Of asphodel, that greeny flower,

        I come, my sweet,

                to sing to you!

My heart rouses

       thinking to bring you news

          of something

that concerns you

       and concerns many men. Look at

          what passes for the new.

You will not find it there but in

       despised poems.

          It is difficult

to get the news from poems

       yet men die miserably every day

          for lack

of what is found there.

       Hear me out

          for I too am concerned

and every man

       who wants to die at peace in his bed

          besides.

PART TWO

THEOCRITUS · IDYL I

A VERSION FROM THE GREEK

THEOCRITUS · IDYL I

THYRSIS

    The whisper of the wind in

        that pine-tree,

           goat-herd,

  is sweet as the murmur of live water;

      likewise

          your flutenotes. After Pan

  you will bear away second prize.

      And if he

        take the goat,

  with his horns,

      the she-goat

        is yours; but if

  he choose the she-goat,

      the kid will fall

        to your lot.

  And the flesh of the kid

      is dainty

        before they begin milking them.

GOAT-HERD

  Your song is sweeter,

    shepherd,

      than the music

of the water as it plashes

    from the high face

        of that rock!

If the Muses

    choose the young ewe

        you shall receive

a stall-fed lamb

    as your reward,

        but if

they prefer the lamb

    you

        shall have the ewe for

        second prize.

THYRSIS

Will you not, goat-herd,

    in the Nymph's name

        take your place on this

        sloping knoll

among the tamarisks

    and pipe for me

        while I tend my sheep.

GOAT-HERD

No, shepherd,

nothing doing;

it's not for us

to be heard during the noon hush.

We dread Pan,

who for a fact

is stretched out somewhere,

dog tired from the chase;

his mood is bitter,

anger ready at his nostrils.

But, Thyrsis,

since you are good at

singing of *The Afflictions of Daphnis,*

and have most deeply

meditated the pastoral mode,

come here,

let us sit down,

under this elm

facing Priapus and the fountain fairies,

here where the shepherds come

to try themselves out

by the oak trees.

          Ah! may you sing

               as you sang that day

facing Chromis out of Libya,

          I will let you milk, yes,

               three times over,

a goat that is the mother of twins

          and even when

               she has sucked her kids

her milk fills

          two pails. I will give besides,

               new made, a two eared bowl

of ivy-wood,

          rubbed with beeswax

               that smacks still

of the knife of the carver.

          Round its upper edges

               winds the ivy, ivy

strewn with yellow flowers

          and about it

               is twisted

a tendril joyful with the saffron fruit.

          Within,

               is limned a girl,

as fair a thing as the gods have made,

dressed in a sweeping

gown.

Her hair

is confined in a snood.

Beside her

two blond-haired youths

with alternate speech

are contending

but her heart is

untouched.

Now,

she glances at one,

smiling,

and now, lightly

she flings the other a thought,

while their eyes,

by reason of love's

long vigils, are heavy

but their labors

all in vain.

In addition

there is fashioned there

an ancient fisherman

and a rock,

    a rugged rock,

        on which

with might and main

    the old man poises a great net

        for the cast

as one who puts his whole heart into it.

    One would say

        that he was fishing

with the full strength of his limbs

    so big do his muscles stand out

        about the neck.

Gray haired though he be,

    he has the strength

        of a young man.

Now, separated

    from the sea-broken old man

        by a narrow interval

is a vineyard,

    heavy

        with fire-red clusters,

and on a rude wall

    sits a small boy

        guarding them.

Round him

       two she-foxes are skulking.

          One

goes the length of the vine-rows

      to eat the grapes

           while the other

brings all her cunning to bear,

      by what has been set down,

         vowing

she will never quit the lad

      until

          she leaves him bare

and breakfastless.

      But the boy

         is plaiting a pretty

cage of locust stalks and asphodel,

      fitting in the reeds

         and cares less for his scrip

and the vines

      than he takes delight

         in his plaiting.

All about the cup

      is draped the mild acanthus,

         a miracle of varied work,

a thing for you to marvel at.

       I paid

            a Caledonian ferry man

a goat and a great white

      cream-cheese

         for the bowl.

It is still virgin to me,

       its lip has never touched mine.

          To gain my desire,

I would gladly

      give this cup

         if you, my friend,

will sing for me

      that delightful song.

         I hold nothing back.

Begin, my friend,

      for you cannot,

        you may be sure,

take your song,

      which drives all things out of mind,

         with you to the other world.

PART THREE

THE DESERT MUSIC

Poem given at the Harvard Assembly in June, 1951,

subsequent to which Dr. Williams was awarded an

honorary Phi Beta Kappa membership.

THE DESERT MUSIC

— the dance begins: to end about a form
propped motionless — on the bridge
between Juarez and El Paso — unrecognizable
in the semi-dark

                  Wait!

The others waited while you inspected it,
on the very walk itself   .

                Is it alive?

                          — neither a head,

legs nor arms!

            It isn't a sack of rags someone
has abandoned here   .   torpid against
the flange of the supporting girder   .   ?

                    an inhuman shapelessness,
knees hugged tight up into the belly

        Egg-shaped!

What a place to sleep!
on the International Boundary.   Where else,
interjurisdictional, not to be disturbed?

How shall we get said what must be said?

Only the poem.

Only the counted poem, to an exact measure:
to imitate, not to copy nature, not
to copy nature

NOT, prostrate, to copy nature

but a dance! to dance
two and two with him —

sequestered there asleep,

right end up!

A music
supersedes his composure, hallooing to us
across a great distance   .   .

wakens the dance
who blows upon his benumbed fingers!

                         Only the poem

only the made poem, to get said what must

be said, not to copy nature, sticks

in our throats   .

The law?   The law gives us nothing

but a corpse, wrapped in a dirty mantle.

The law is based on murder and confinement,

long delayed,

but this, following the insensate music,

is based on the dance:

                    an agony of self realization

bound into a whole

by that which surrounds us   .

                         I cannot escape

I cannot vomit it up

Only the poem!

Only the made poem, the verb calls it

                         into being.

— it looks too small for a man.
A woman.   Or a very shriveled old man.
Maybe dead.   They probably inspect the place
and will cart it away later   .

Heave it into the river.
A good thing.

Leaving California to return east, the fertile desert,
                    (were it to get water)
surrounded us, a music of survival, subdued, distant, half
                    heard; we were engulfed
by it as in the early evening, seeing the wind lift
                    and drive the sand, we
passed Yuma. All night long, heading for El Paso to
                    meet our friend,
we slept fitfully.   Thinking of Paris, I waked to the tick
                    of the rails.   The
jagged desert   .

                    — to tell
what subsequently I saw and what heard

        — to place myself (in

my nature) beside nature

        — to imitate

nature (for to copy nature would be a

    shameful thing)

       I lay myself down:

The Old Market's a good place to begin:

Let's cut through here —

         techilla's only

a nickel a slug in these side streets.

Keep out though.   Oh, it's all right at

this time of day but I saw H. terribly

beaten up in one of those joints.   He

asked for it.   I thought he was going to

be killed.   I do

my drinking on the main drag   .

     That's the bull-ring

Oh, said Floss, after she got used to the
change of light   .

                        What color!   Isn't it
wonderful!

            — paper flowers (para los santos)
baked red-clay utensils, daubed
with blue, silverware,
dried peppers, onions, print goods, children's
clothing   .   the place deserted all but
for a few Indians squatted in the
booths, unnoticing (don't you think it)
as though they slept there   .

        There's a second tier.   Do you
want to go up?

        What makes Texans so tall?
We saw a woman this morning in a mink cape
six feet if she was an inch.   What a woman!

Probably a Broadway figure.

— tell you what else we saw: about a million
sparrows screaming their heads off
in the trees of that small park where
the buses stop, sanctuary,
I suppose,
from the wind driving the sand in that way
about the city   .

                              Texas rain they call it

— and those two alligators in the fountain   .

There were four

                   I saw only two

                            They were looking
right at you all the time   .

Penny please!   Give me penny please, mister.

                    Don't give them anything.

.   instinctively
one has already drawn one's naked
wrist away from those obscene fingers
as in the mind a vague apprehension speaks
and the music rouses   .

Let's get in here.
a music!   cut off as
the bar door closes behind us.

We've got
another half hour.

— returned to the street,
the pressure moves from booth to booth along
the curb.   Opposite, no less insistent
the better stores are wide open.   Come in
and look around.   You don't have to buy: hats,
riding boots, blankets   .

Look at the way,
slung from her neck with a shawl, that young
Indian woman carries her baby!

                    — a stream of Spanish,
as she brushes by, intense, wide-
eyed in eager talk with her boy husband

— three half-grown girls, one of them eating a
pomegranate.   Laughing.

                        and the serious tourist,
man and wife, middle aged, middle western,
their arms loaded with loot, whispering
together — still looking for bargains   .

                        and the aniline
red and green candy at the little booth
tended by the old Indian woman.
            Do you suppose anyone actually
buys — and eats the stuff?

My feet are beginning to ache me.

                    We still got a few minutes.
Let's try here.   They had the mayor
up last month for taking $3000 a week from

the whore houses of the city.   Not much left
for the girls.   There's a show on.

                    Only a few tables
occupied.   A conventional orchestra — this
place livens up later — playing the usual local
jing-a-jing — — a boy and girl team, she
                    confidential with someone
off stage.   Laughing: just finishing the act.

So we drink until the next turn — a strip tease.

Do you mean it?   Wow!   Look at her.

                    You'd have to be
pretty drunk to get any kick out of that.
She's no Mexican.   Some worn out trouper from
the States.   Look at those breasts   .

            There is a fascination
            seeing her shake
            the beaded sequins from
            a string about her hips

She gyrates but it's
not what you think,
one does not laugh
to watch her belly.

One is moved but not
at the dull show.   The
guitarist yawns.   She
cannot even sing.   She

has about her painted
hardihood a screen
of pretty doves which
flutter their wings.

Her cold eyes perfunct-
orily moan but do not
smile.   Yet they bill
and coo by grace of
a certain candor.   She

is heavy on her feet.
That's good.   She

                    bends forward leaning
                    on the table of the
                    balding man sitting
                    upright, alone, so that
                    everything hangs for-
                    ward.
                            What the hell

                    are you grinning
                    to yourself about?   Not
                    at *her*?
                            The music!
                    I like her.   She fits

                    the music   .

Why don't these Indians get over this nauseating prattle
about their souls and their loves and sing us something
else for a change?

                    This place is rank
                    with it.   She
                    at least knows she's
                    part of another tune,

knows her customers,
has the same
opinion of them as I
have.   That gives her
one up   .   one up
following the lying
music   .

There is another music.   The bright colored candy
of her nakedness lifts her unexpectedly
to partake of its tune   .

                              Andromeda of those rocks,
the virgin of her mind   .   those unearthly
greens and reds

                              in her mockery of virtue
she becomes unaccountably virtuous   .
                            though she in no
way pretends it   .

Let's get out of this.

In the street it hit
me in the face as we started to walk again.   Or
am I merely playing the poet?   Do I merely invent
it out of whole cloth?   I thought   .

What in the form of an old whore in
a cheap Mexican joint in Juarez, her bare
can waggling crazily can be
so refreshing to me, raise to my ear
so sweet a tune, built of such slime?

Here we are.   They'll be along any minute.
The bar is at the right of the entrance,
a few tables opposite which you have to pass
to get to the dining room, beyond.

A foursome, two oversize Americans, no
longer young, got up as cow-boys,
hats and all, are drunk and carrying on
with their gals, drunk also,

especially one inciting her man, the
biggest, *Yip ee!* to dance in

the narrow space, oblivious to everything
— she is insatiable and he is trying

stumblingly to keep up with her.
Give it the gun, pardner! *Yip ee*! We
pushed by them to our table, seven
of us.   Seated about the room

were quiet family groups, some with
children, eating.   Rather a better
class than you notice
on the streets.   So here we are.   You

can see through into the kitchen
where one of the cooks, his shirt sleeves
rolled up, an apron over
the well pressed pants of a street

suit, black hair neatly parted,
a tall
good looking man, is working
absorbed, before a chopping block

Old fashioneds all around?

                                    So this is William
Carlos Williams, the poet   .

                                    Floss and I had half consumed
our quartered hearts of lettuce before
we noticed the others hadn't touched theirs   .
You seem quite normal.   Can you tell me?   Why
does one want to write a poem?

                            Because it's there to be written.

Oh.   A matter of inspiration then?

                                                Of necessity.

Oh.   But what sets it off?

                            I am that he whose brains
                            are scattered
                                    aimlessly

                                    — and so,
the hour done, the quail eaten, we were on
our way back to El Paso.

                        Good night.   Good
night and thank you   .   No.   Thank you.   We're
going to walk   .

— and so, on the naked wrist, we feel again
those insistent fingers   .

                        Penny please, mister.
Penny please.   Give me penny.

                        Here! now go away.

— but the music, the music has reawakened
as we leave the busier parts of the street
and come again to the bridge in the semi-dark,
pay our fee and begin again to cross   .
seeing the lights along the mountain back of El
Paso and pause to watch the boys calling out
to us to throw more coins to them standing

in the shallow water   .   so that's
where the incentive lay, with the annoyance
of those surprising fingers.

                    So you're a poet?
a good thing to be got rid of — half drunk,
a free dinner under your belt, even though you
get typhoid — and to have met people you
can at least talk to   .

            relief from that changeless, endless
inescapable and insistent music   .

            What else, Latins, do you yourselves
seek but relief!
with the expressionless ding dong you dish up
to us of your souls and your loves, which
we swallow. Spaniards! (though these are mostly
Indians who chase the white bastards
through the streets on their Independence Day
and try to kill them)   .

                        What's that?

Oh, come on.

But what's THAT?

                     the music! the
music!   as when Casals struck
and held a deep cello tone
and I am speechless   .

                    There it sat
in the projecting angle of the bridge flange
as I stood aghast and looked at it —
in the half light: shapeless or rather returned
to its original shape, armless, legless,
headless, packed like the pit of a fruit into
that obscure corner — or
a fish to swim against the stream — or
a child in the womb prepared to imitate life,
warding its life against
a birth of awful promise.   The music
guards it, a mucus, a film that surrounds it,
a benumbing ink that stains the
sea of our minds — to hold us off — shed

of a shape close as it can get to no shape,
a music! a protecting music   .

                    I *am* a poet! I
am.   I am.   I am a poet, I reaffirmed, ashamed

Now the music volleys through as in
a lonely moment I hear it.   Now it is all
about me.   The dance!   The verb detaches itself
seeking to become articulate   .

           And I could not help thinking
           of the wonders of the brain that
           hears that music and of our
           skill sometimes to record it.